Stories of Three Unique Years

World War II - U.S. Army Memories of a 100 Year Old Veteran

Henry Schueftan

Dedication

I dedicate this book to my late wife of many years Ruth Schueftan.

Thank You

I had a great deal of help from staff at Mather Pavillion and Symphony of Evanston, which I deeply appreciate.

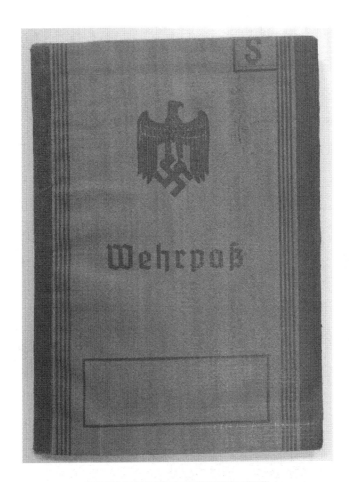

Military Passport

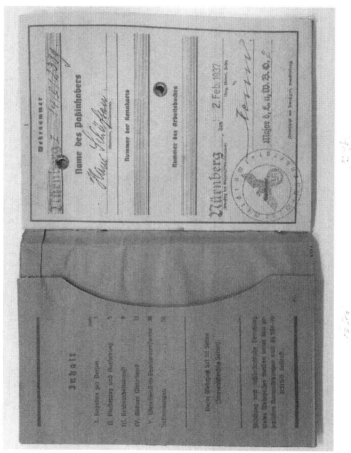

Table of Contents

Foreword

1. From Private Citizen to Private in the U.S. Army
2. Not a Good Day
3. It is Not Easy to Observe One's Religious Rites
4. A Freshly Minted US Citizen
5. An Unusual Reception
6. Life in Fort Benjamin Harrison
7. General Rommel's Afrika Corps
8. Army Specialized Training Program
9. The Foreign Physical
10. This Could Have Ended Badly
11. Shipping Out
12. Not Quite a Civilian
13. A Change of Scenery
14. Criqueville
15. Operational Area
16. From G-11 Analyst to Clerk (and Driver)
17. Baptism of Fire
18. A "Restroom" Crisis
19. Alcohol and Anti-Semitism
20. Impressive Power
21. Crash of a U.S. Fighter Plane

22. Signs of the Times – In France 1945
23. Paris
24. Loss of a British Bomber
25. Hollywood on Temporary Duty
26. A Different Shower
27. Jalhay, Belgium
28. Town of EU, Belgium
29. A Case of Duress – Nice Try!
30. Yes Virginia, There is a SPA
31. Death of FDR
32. A Rebuilt Synagogue and Pope Benedict XVI
33. Visiting my Father's Grave
34. Weimar and Buchenwald
35. It Still Sounded German
36. In Vino Veritas
37. A Personal Pilgrimage
38. The German Dentist Before Denazification
39. Our Last Stop in Germany
40. Going Home Step #1
41. SS Frederic 12,000 Tons
42. Your Dog Will Always Know You
43. No 90 Days Wonders There

Epilogue

Foreword

I was born on November 12, 1914, in Berlin, Germany (at that time Charlottenburg, before the creation of "Great Berlin" in 1924.) My family never lived in Berlin, a fact that perhaps requires some explanation. My parents at that time lived in a small town in Bavaria, southern Germany. When my mother was expecting (me!) she traveled to Warsaw, Poland, with my older sister to visit her parents. Some months before November, World War I broke out; there was no possibility for her to go back using the shortest route. Therefore, my mother took a train going north, then to Berlin by way of Copenhagen, Denmark, where she was met by my father. My somewhat early appearance resulted in my mother checking into a women's private clinic. This made me the only sibling of three to be born in a hospital. The hospital wound up in the American Zone of Occupation, and was destroyed in WWII. At the time the Nazi government took over, we lived in Nuremberg – a place which has entered history books with a good deal of negative "baggage."

My father was a manufacturer's representative, selling edible fats on commission. From 1925-1932 he operated a small movie theater in downtown Nuremberg. When he closed the theater, he resumed his old occupation. By the time he died in July 1935 he had found a few good firms to represent. It should be mentioned here that two of the firms, Christian-German owned, continued paying commissions to me on repeat business, a very decent action indeed. My mother followed me one year after my arrival. During that year these firms continued paying commissions to my mother. I have tried to contact them to express my appreciation but they were no longer in business.

Another matter deserves to be recalled. At the time I left Germany I was employed by an export company, in charge of shipping. When leaving I had a rather large wooden crate for my baggage which I had picked up by Schenker & Co., an international shipping company. When informed about this shipment my contactman (we used the firm extensively) expressed his regret about my leaving, and also – a nice gesture – there will be no invoice. It felt good to have your faith somewhat restored.

Being only 22 years old, I had a mid-level office job after a two year apprenticeship. Due to the gradual elimination of Jews from economic life, there was no future for Jews to stay in Germany. In addition, there were great risks (so conclusively proved later on), and Nuremberg, with its arch anti-Semite Julius Streicher, was no longer a good place to live. Therefore, I called on a distant relative in Chicago for help, to furnish an affidavit of support. This was needed under the law at that time to make sure that the future immigrant would not become a burden on the public welfare system. The affidavit of support arrived almost by return mail, which in those days was one full month. My appointment with the consulate in Stuttgart did not end well. My application was rejected. In 1935 I tried again – same result. At the end of 1936, with additional affidavits from other relatives, success came my way. I arrived in Chicago on April 10th, 1937, after I had lived in Nazi Germany more than 4 years.

Of course, it was my intention to become a U.S. Citizen. I applied just short of the necessary five years, and was given a date to appear with two witnesses who had known me the full five years – this took some effort. I had met both of them while living in the Hyde Park Y after my arrival in Chicago. After I had passed the oral examination I was told that I would get the certificate in the mail. When the Certificate failed to arrive after a reasonable time, I called Immigration and Naturalization to learn the reason for the delay. I was told that as a German National I was considered an enemy alien; the department had stopped all naturalizations of that group. There was still the matter of the draft, having previously registered, and having received #1230 in the ensuing lottery. After a long interval of a few weeks, I was informed that I had to fill out a form answering some personal questions. I was required to indicate any organizations of which I was a member, omitting those that reflected one's religion. The form closed with the question: "are you willing to serve in the armed forces?" Ominously it stated that if one answered "no," one could never be naturalized. My answer was "Yes." Soon after, on January 9th, 1943, I was inducted into the U.S. Army. As to my naturalization, I was told to apply while in the Army via an accelerated procedure.

This book is not intended to be a biography of my Army service. To some extent, it reports on the Army's functioning on a detachment level, and also reports episodes which are more of a personal nature. My army service was a little more than three years, and, as it was so different from my previous life, it becomes a reportable object. I was not an officer; I was a "noncom," a noncommissioned officer, a Staff sergeant. Noncoms are also called enlisted men (even if they did not enlist), S/Sgt is one of the three highest enlisted ranks, and it is a good rank, not just for the extra money. The first three grades get more respect, both from the lower enlisted ranks as well as from the officers.

If you, dear reader, served in any of the armed forces, I am sure you will see some of your own experiences confirmed. If you did not serve, I hope that it will give you some idea about being a member of the U.S. Armed Forces.

1) I graduated with a B.S.B.A. from Northwestern University, Chicago, Illinois, in 1955.

2) Contrary to the impression you may have, I did not keep a diary while in the Service. I am blessed (!?) with total recall. My memory is as sharp as ever.

3) When Germany instituted the draft, the thinking in their army was that anyone otherwise qualified should be drafted. Therefore, as I was in the age range, I had to report for a physical examination on February 2nd, 1937. I was judged to be "tauglich II," or limited service. This is exactly the classification I received when I reported for the draft in the United States. It is interesting to note that both Armies had the same opinion of my fitness for service. Ultimately, Jews were not drafted into the Germany army.

Chapter 1: From Private Citizen to Private in the U.S. Army

I reported to the Draft Board on Hyde Park Boulevard early in the morning of 1/9/1943. There were about fifty other draftees. A bus took us to the old B&O Railroad station on Dearborn near Harris Street. A train then took us to Camp Grant, located near Rockford. There we were assigned a bed in a barrack, and some of the men were issued their uniforms and other clothes. However, it was too late for the crew there to service all of us, and at the end of the day I still found myself walking around in my "civies", and feeling somewhat uncomfortable. This had an unforeseen consequence; the men wearing uniforms were given passes to go to Rockford, while the others had to stay in camp. The next morning, after breakfast, we were issued uniforms, and under guidance, prepared to send our regular clothes home. Later in the day, perhaps forty of us boarded a train and traveled to Fort Benjamin Harrison, Indiana, about 12 miles northeast of downtown Indianapolis, Indiana.

My life in the army had begun.

Chapter 2: Not a Good Day

After joining the U.S. Army there are two things that are ahead of you. Your spectacles (eyes) are checked, and…. There is the dentist. I reported to the dental clinic, and a major peered into my mouth. "You still have your wisdom teeth," he announced. My somewhat meek reply – "they have not bothered me." He had an answer for that: "But they may at the wrong time." There were three teeth. My fate was sealed.

The major turned me over to another dentist who gave me what I think was a large dosage of Novocain or similar medicine. Three molars came out, two lower and one upper one. That dentist showed no mercy, as my ticket, to be returned to the orderly room, read disposition

"Duty." I had absolutely no control over the lower part of my face. I entered the First Sergeant's office. He looked at the ticket, and looked at my face; it softened his regular army heart of perhaps fifteen years service, and he said, "You better lie down until lunch." I did manage to be off duty until the evening meal. I could not eat and the Novocain's effect lasted almost until late afternoon.

Chapter 3: It is Not Easy to Observe One's Religious Rites

Fort Benjamin Harrison, Indiana, where I had my basic training (Basic Infantry and Finance School) had an interdenominational chapel. It was prepared to reflect both the Christian and Jewish religions, as required. Therefore, on a Friday evening, the time of the services, I asked the First Sergeant for permission to attend, another man also joining me in this request. Friday night was the time of the big clean-up, which presented a conflict. The answer I received was that I should take the request to my squad-leader, which I did just before the clean-up was to start. "Now," he said, putting on an utterly fair face, "It would not be fair to these other guys, if you went off to church, while they are working their butts off. There is a coal pile at the cellar window of the building. After you two shovel it in, you can go."

I had been part of doing this job before. Usually there are ten men and five shovels, so that half of the men can take a break. It was about 25 degrees, with light snow. We both started shoveling, but my buddy gave up after about ten minutes. I, perhaps foolishly, carried on until I completed the job really exhausted. I did go to services; I enjoyed the post-services snack of Corned Beef Sandwiches, brought in by the ladies of an Indianapolis congregation.

The following week I had a terrible cold and went on sick-call. Having no temperature over 100 degrees, I was prescribed a throat swab. During my whole army life, I was never hospitalized.

Chapter 4: A Freshly Minted U.S. Citizen

After a few weeks in Fort Benjamin Harrison, Indiana, I went to see the Post Naturalization Officer who helped me to fill out my application. It was sent to the Federal District Court in Cincinnati, Ohio, because the court in Indianapolis has no naturalization judge. In February I was notified that the judge would not come to Indy until June, as I had missed the January court date. A few days before the June date, I went to see the First Sergeant of my company, as it was required that I be accompanied by two non-commissioned officers who could confirm that I was indeed a member of the armed forces. While there, the head of the company, a captain, by chance entered the office and asked what this was all about. After being informed, he turned to me and asked a few questions – where was I from? How long had I had been in the country? Etc. He then told me that the following Saturday he was supposed to speak to the whole company, about 220 men, on "Why We Fight." Would I like to speak to the company? I agreed to do so.

It was a heady experience; I, practically a rookie, speaking to men of all ranks and a good number of officers. I spoke extemporaneously for about forty-five minutes, followed by a fifteen minute period for questions. Let me make an interesting observation: when one is in basic training, it is advisable that one's name does not become a household word. Rather, it is better for one to just blend into the woodwork. If you are well known, you probably get more work. But – the deed was done, and my story became palpable to the rest of the company.

June of 1943 came, and I showed up in court in downtown Indianapolis with two corporals. The soldiers to be naturalized were sitting in the jury box, while others sat in the section for the public. Of course, before returning to camp I treated my entourage to drinks at a bar in the area.

It was a happy day.

Chapter 5: An Unusual Reception

Part of basic training in Fort Benjamin Harrison, Indiana, was attending classes in Finance School. The instructors were noncoms, noncommissioned officers, usually staff sergeants. During that period they were replaced by just commissioned Second Lieutenants. Also during that time we were given a three hour test called OCT-1. I do now know if the Army had plans to use it, or was just testing the test. It covered the following fields: Mechanics, General Science, Language Skills (developing a new language,) and General Education. It took place in the Headquarters Building. A few weeks later I was told to come to a reception at Headquarters. The reception was for the newly installed second Lieutenants.

In addition to the second Lieutenants, the reception was attended by the school's officers, the commanding officer, the master sergeant or sergeant major of headquarters, and myself. OF course, I felt pretty much out of place.

It took me some time to find out why I was invited – I had the highest score in the OCT-1 test.

Chapter 6: Life in Fort Benjamin Harrison, Indiana

When non-army people talk about the army, we frequently hear the adage: "NEVER VOLUNTEER." I have violated this principal many times – to volunteer, when possible, for the tolerable task rather than finding yourself required to do something that you do not like to do.

After basic training, I was assigned to be part of the cadre, the permanent personnel. In this position I would work at personnel, processing the records of inductees coming into the Finance Replacement Training Center.

One thing I learned early on: my first Sunday in the Army, I was fully dressed at 8.00 A.M. This was the morning someone rounded me up; I was cleaning Theater #1, and had never seen so much popcorn in my life.

Another Sunday I found myself working in the office because the Colonel wanted to make a change. This happened to me only once, as the next weekend I got a two day pass, went to Indianapolis on Saturday, stayed at the "YMCA" for 50 cents, and returned Sunday evening. A buddy from Ohio, who became a good friend of mine, joined me, and we had a regular routine. Sunday morning we went to a certain church for breakfast. We went to the movies on Sunday afternoon on Monument Circle, and Sunday evening we both went to a Jewish center, the Kirschbaum Center, for supper. The latter was quite democratic; Army officers went there too. Once a month I went home, taking the Monon railroad. It was a four hour ride for 180 miles, the milk run. It was supposed to be back by 6:00 A.M. Sunday, but it never made it before 7.00 A.M. When the train left the station, the conductor began writing excuse tickets, because as long as it was scheduled to be back at the time noted on the pass, one was in the clear.

A case of Meningitis kept us restricted to the post for a month. After a number of months I became restless and looked for change. When the opportunity arose, I applied for the Army Specialized Training Program.

Chapter 7: General Romney's Africa Corps

It was a hot summer day when I was summoned to see the First Sergeant. I was shown a piece of note paper, on which was written a relatively simple sentence in German: "Wir Holen Deutsche P.O.W.'s vom schiff ab und bringen sie in ein Lager." I was supposed to travel with an M.P. (Military Police) unit to New Jersey to pick up German prisoners of war. After translating it from the German, I was told to join the M.P. unit the next day, with baggage for a week. This was rather a clever move on the part of the Army; some men listed German as a fluent language, when they could barely say or understand the simplest phrase.

The train, which we boarded in the evening, had an old locomotive, a tender, a dining car, ten day coaches, each for fifty men, with the windows blocked, and a Pullman sleeping car for the troops and a doctor. The M.P. company, a physician, and I got off in Bayonne, New Jersey. Our charges were not to arrive until midnight; we had to look for our own food in the meantime. There was not much of a choice at the nearby station, and we emptied the bakery very quickly. At midnight the prisoners came aboard. They were a somewhat bedraggled lot. We travelled rather slowly while avoiding major cities. The prisoners were provided with very simple food.

My duties were threefold. I had to prepare a list of their names, and make announcements as instructed by the M.P. officers. As there was no speaker system, I had to speak twice in each coach. I also had to make the rounds with the doctor each morning, translating their symptoms and health complaints. The doctor had an ironic sense of humor. One very young man had a skin complaint. Looking at the site, the doctor asked how long he had been experiencing the affliction. "Since I came to Africa," the young man explained. "Then tell your people to keep out of Africa," the doctor suggested. Another medical event occurred near St. Louis, Missouri. One of the prisoners had abdominal pains, and the doctor suspected Appendicitis. He wired ahead for an ambulance to pick up the patient at a station in the St. Louis area. In spite of his pains, before entering the vehicle, the patient stood at attention and saluted. We also had a malaria patient, but no quinine. He was shaking with frost, lying flat on two seats, all covered with blankets.

The trip was not a pleasure trip by anyone's imagination. Going south, it was extremely hot with no air conditioning, so the windows were open only in the coaches not used by the prisoners, and everyone was exposed to the smoke and soot of the coal burning equipment. After more than five days we arrived in Camp Livingston near Shreveport, Louisiana. Tthere was only one thought in the train personnels' minds – a clean bed and shower. This was half promised by the officers. However, after the prisoners were turned over to the local guards, our hopes were rudely dashed. Train management decided that the train had to return to Indianapolis immediately. There was almost a riot, as our guards were quite angry. Some ten hours later we arrived in Fort Benjamin Harrison, Indiana. Getting off the train I had rubber legs – a condition well known to people riding trains for a long time.

I did not enjoy this trip but it was a good experience.

Chapter 8: ASTP - Army Specialized Training Program

In June of 1943 the Army instituted the ASTP, the Army Specialized Training Program. It was not a success. It would involve taking courses at certain colleges; one could apply, and the application would be judged based on one's education. I applied and was accepted.

My first stop was, at that time, CCNY, New York. We were housed in what used to be a Jewish Orphanage on 134th Street and Amsterdam Avenue. It was a building with too few normal toilets and a great number of miniature ones. It seems that the program had not yet been fully developed, so we actually did not do much beyond our own housekeeping. The food was catered. We rotated among the men, each one off 48 hours and on 24 hours. I had a cousin living in Great Neck, Long Island at that time. I spent a lot of time out three, and in those days, when returning to New York, I never had a chance to take a train. Someone always picked me up on the way.

New York was a great soldiers' town. The Stage Door Canteen was a disappointment, but at 99 Park Avenue we could pick up leftover Broadway theater tickets for free at 1 PM on weekdays. I think it was in November of 1943 when we were ordered to participate in the Navy Day festivities. We marched about 35 blocks down Fifth Avenue. Being a Corporal, I was the pivot man. It should be noted that people living around Broadway and Amsterdam Avenue were quite upset, because a live bugler blew reveille every morning. Around November 1 I received travel orders, to the University of Illinois in Urbana, Illinois. There were about thirty men in my group.

After arriving there we found out that we were to live in the Phi Kappa Psi Frat house. Soon after a lieutenant called, "Who is the ranking man?" "We have a corporal here," was the answer. That was me. When I talked to the officer, he told me that a) I was to be in charge of the group, and b) that I was Cadet Lieutenant. Well, I did what was done in this situation. Rank has its privileges; I took the powder-room on the ground floor, while the rest of the men took the dormer. All of us were language specialists; specific instructions were not considered necessary. We had to take one course, and spend time in a cubicle in the library. Food was catered in the nearby Armory. We also had to have close order drill in the armory. My guys would have cheerfully obeyed my command to walk into a wall, but I managed to keep them free of injuries. There were a number of other platoons there having a close order drill in the same area. A Major watched me giving the commands and said to me, "That was pretty good, Corporal." After a number of weeks we were transferred to other camps for taking courses. We went to Camp Crowder in Missouri's southwest corner, and Vint Hill Farms Station near Warrenton, Virginia, closed when the intelligence community was consolidated. The program did not last that long – it was discontinued after only a matter of months. I never saw an official explanation for its discontinuance. I would guess the higher ups concluded that by the time they could get benefits from it, the war would be over, and they needed the men. It was simply not worth the planning and operating expense.

I am quite sure that the orphanage in New York was torn down in the meantime.

Chapter 9: The Foreign Physical

When there is a possibility that somebody is going to be "shipped" overseas, he is given what is called a foreign physical. I was stationed at the University of Illinois at the time, when I was called to Chanute Field, Illinois, for my foreign physical.

The doctor checked various areas, including heart and lungs. Lastly, he checked my blood pressure. It was somewhat elevated, and I actually had a chance to avoid foreign service, if I would choose to. However, there were a number of factors that caused me not to go this route. When one's unit ships out and one is separated from it, all kind of unpleasant things can happen. One can be sent to a so-called casual company. One loses the friends which one has made while in the service. Besides, one can wind up doing work that one detests. Furthermore, I had not seen my sister and brother, living in what is now Israel, for more than nine years, and I nursed the quiet hope that somehow, should my tour of duty take me to Europe, it would be possible for me to visit them. Actually, this did become reality, which I will report on later.

For these reasons, I asked the doctor to let me lie down for a little while, and he complied with my suggestion. So foreign service was in my cards. I passed the physical.

Chapter 10: This Could Have Ended Badly

I spent some time in MacDill Field, Florida, between assignments. One day I was told to clean up the gym with another man. I was a corporal and he was a private. Arriving at the gym, I was about to look for someone to give us our tools and instructions when my buddy piped up, "Don't be an eager beaver, let them look for us!" I did not feel quite good about doing this but went along. When we reported back to the First Sergeant, he asked, "Where were you fellows all day?" I answered that we had been at the gym but nobody told us what to do. "Well," he said, "the gym people are sore. You better go back tomorrow morning."

The next morning found us back at the gym. I was going to look for somebody, when my "friend" again took the same tack. This time I went my own way, and swept and mopped the place, grudgingly assisted by my colleague.

Chapter 11: Shipping Out

I had the good fortune to go to Europe, not by way of a crowded troopship like the French liner Normandie, but by air. We travelled in a four engine C54, with the TWA insignia painted over in dark brown. Ours was a group of about thirty men who had spent time together in various training venues. Our paperwork was processed in a permanent camp in the Washington D.C. area, and we took off from a military airport in the same area. For most of us it may have been the first flight ever, but after a short time, everyone behaved as if it was just another bus ride.

Having a window seat, I noticed something red hot in one of the engines. The crew reassured me that it was just the manifold, and I relaxed. We flew at about 220 miles per hour. At 12,000 feet altitude what I saw looking down was breath-taking. At about 10:00 PM we touched down in Newfoundland for refueling. We walked to the terminal, shivering in the cool night temperature, while wearing our Florida summer uniforms. After another six hour flight, we arrived in Prestwick, Scotland. A bus took us to Glasgow, and there we boarded a train with rows of metal bunk beds, two high. There was no privacy; one did not undress. Blankets were furnished, and one removed one's jacket and topcoat. A new experience – rather practical, and I am sure much cheaper than a Pullman sleeper.

Chapter 12: Not Quite a Civilian

After our arrival in London, we pitched our tents near Ascot Racetrack for a few days before traveling to Maidstone, County of Kent. In Maidstone the unexpected happened: we were to attend an Intelligence course given by the Royal Air Force at a nearby location, and, there being no Army installation in the area, we were to board with families.

My quarters were with a very nice British family, whose son was in the British Army and whose room I used. The family was paid by the U.S. Army. We had to take a bus to the facility; the lady of the house, Mrs. Brennan, packed a lunch for me. In the evening my colleagues and I could go either to the movies or to a pub. On June 6, 1944 the invasion of Europe (France) by Allied Forces began.

Nothing remained the same.

Chapter 13: A Change of Scenery

After we left Maidstone we went to a camp north of London. There was a water pipe problem, and we were not able to take showers during the last ten days. At the end of June, we went to Portsmouth on the southern coast to board a ship for France. I have no idea how this problem started, but when we arrived at the port there was no ship! It seems that somehow we got there late. Our answer to what to do has been done for centuries; we waited for the next ship.

Where did we wait? Outdoors of course, right by the pier. Four long days. I slept either on the ground, or a bench in the area, until one of my more enterprising buddies discovered some folding cots. Luckily it did not rain at all. We were given C-ration cans and ate donuts and drank coffee at a nearby Red Cross hut. By the time the ship arrived, we had not taken a shower for two weeks, and that's all anybody could think of. That four day crossing of the canal was worlds apart from the new fast trains between France and the United Kingdom. We took a zigzag route, and the ship took its time.

We were still getting C-rations, a monotonous diet. One day I watched some navy men through a window eating lunch. My hungry look was noticed by one of the men, who obviously had a soft heart for army men. He came out and asked if I wanted a steak sandwich. Did I ever!!! This was the best meal I had had in weeks. Moreover, when using the restroom, I saw a shower stall inside. The navy man, whom I asked if I could use it, mentioned that it was seawater. He told me I should not mention him if the Navy Officer quizzed me. "How is he going to know I am not in the Navy?" I asked flippantly. In all the excitement about finally taking a shower, I forgot that I had no towel. Just then, a buddy of mine entered, which turned out to be a blind alley. He refused to get a towel for me, asking, "Why should you take a shower when nobody else can?" My reply: "They can all use it if they want to take a chance getting chewed out by the officer." Still no dice. There was only one thing to do – use the quite dirty shower curtain.

Using this kind of water makes one's skin feel very clammy. And after that shower, I almost felt that I need another one. I generally do not hold a grudge, but in this case I made an exception. In due time we arrived at what is known as Omaha Beach; I had to go down a rope net on the side of the ship while carrying my duffel-bag, as there was no harbor. A small Navy landing craft took us the last five hundred feet to the beach.

Chapter 14: Criqueville-sur-dessi: Our First Site in France

The site was ringed with the typical Normandie hedgerows, which can be more troublesome than a chain-link fence. There was also a breath of farm life there. A farmer brought a cow in to graze; she was tethered to a chain with a spike in the lawn that he moved every so often. Of course, we had to watch where we stepped.

There I also found a woman to do my "linge" (laundry); I had to furnish the soap, which was GI soup, a jelly.

Chapter 15: Operational Area

At the main area there were operational vans with radio equipment; also the detachment office (called the Orderly Room in Army language), the motor pool, the supply room, the maintenance shop, the radio repair shop, and the cryptographic van. When we were able to move much further inland we had a forward site with direction finding equipment about twelve miles from the main camp.

Chapter 16: From G-II Analyst to Clerk (and Driver)

My training in intelligence took place in many locations. Camp Crowder, Missouri, Vint Hill Farms Station, Virginia, and Sutton Valence near Maidstone, England. I joined my unit near Omaha beach and was promptly put on a work schedule. However, I hardly got my seat warm when the Captain wanted to speak to me. He told me that the detachment had all the intelligence personnel that they needed; what they really needed was a clerk in the orderly room. I was rather disappointed, but I soon realized that my new job had its importance, too. As I was not always busy, I did some driving for the motorpool; this brought a little variety into my life. Furthermore, I did not have guard duty.

In 1945 we received some infantrymen who had psychological problems, similar to problems encountered by our service men in the more recent wars. They were basics, laborers. Their service records were not in good shape, perhaps due to their frequent change of station. This would affect the timing of their return home. It was quite rewarding for me to be able to help them, by updating their records. This surprised them greatly.

Chapter 17: Baptism of Fire

We were not far from Omaha beach, in pyramidal tents and sleeping peacefully. At about midnight, two bombs fell about 1000 feet from our area. The ground shook; I got out on the wrong side of my collapsible bed. The consensus was that it was not enemy action, but, rather, planes on the way to their landing strip dropping their bombs. Perhaps they had damage and this was done for safety. In the morning we found two large holes in the adjacent field, perhaps thirty feet in diameter each. There was a great deal of activity that morning, as a lot of men dug foxholes, making walking around very risky. I myself played the percentages; I did not do any digging. I figured that the chances of a repeat performance were very low.

There were no more bombs at that time.

Chapter 18: A Restroom Crisis

France, near Omaha Beach.

Whenever we moved, it was done in two parts, separated by a few days, so that we could be fully operational all the time. The Captain and the First Sergeant moved with the first group, and I was in charge of the second group. While preparing a new campsite, the first thing which needs to be done is providing "toilet" facilities. If the location is outdoors, a slit trench needs to be dug. This has its drawbacks, but there is no other way. After about a week, we got hold of some lumber, and a carpenter among the men fashioned a primitive but quite useable seat. There was no time to work out a complicated work schedule; I just had to grab anyone and tell him what to do. A few men got the job of filling in the trench.

When removing the various items from the trucks, it occurred to me that I had not seen the seat. When questioned, one of the men said, "We buried it! You didn't tell us to take it along." "Didn't you think that we would need it?" Is all I could say. It was back to square one for about a week.

What did I learn from this event, or rather, non-event? To make one's instructions more complete, even if something seems obvious.

Chapter 19: Alcohol & Anti-Semitism

It was never good news when the detachment got hold of alcoholic beverages. In Normandy, there is a drink called Calvados, a brandy made from apples. It is very potent, and bought from Frenchmen in unlabeled bottles. We almost lost a man to it. The men drank it in the tents. One man had the odd habit of taking a truck out for a drink when drunk; this presented quite a problem. Another man went down a camp path, while shouting "We've got too many Jews in this outfit!" – I heard it myself.

The captain did not hear it, but somehow was informed of the occurrence. The man was transferred to another detachment within a day or two. I was not too surprised by the occurrence; usually cases of anti-Semitism are more subtle.

Chapter 20: Impressive Power

Not far from Omaha Beach near St. Lo, France.

The first time I watched twelve hundred B-24s, also called "Flying Fortresses," flying overhead at about 12,000 feet (there were no jets in those days) it was quite a sight. The cabins were not pressurized, so 12,000 feet was their limit in altitude. If my memory serves me right, they traveled in groups of 12; it was quite noisy and took about half of one hour for the whole armada to pass. About two hours later they returned. Watching them fly overhead, I wondered where they had been for their mission. This event was repeated many times.

Chapter 21: Crash of a U.S. Fighter Plane

We were in Belgium about ten miles from the German frontier, on a sunny Sunday afternoon, when a fighter plane crashed not far from our area. Some of our men rushed to get there, in case the pilot somehow survived, but he had not. I was among the men who brought the remains to the cemetery.

Apparently, he took a hit from German fighter planes or artillery on the German side. When we were given his wallet, I noticed an odd coincidence. It contained a small strip of metal, part of a bracelet, engraved with his name, Los Angeles, and four numbers, perhaps the end of his telephone number. The bracelet said "Dunton 4940." These numbers were the same as the last numbers of my phone number at home. Figuring that I might need this information, I made a note of it. A few months after my return home, I found a phone number in Los Angeles with the same name.

When I called the number, the pilot's Mother answered. I told her that I had been at her son's crash site, and that he had been killed on impact. Of course she had already been informed of his death by the Army, but I wanted to share with her my own understanding of her son's death. A few years later I spent my vacation on the west coast. I contacted her and we met for lunch. She was most appreciative having heard from an eye witness of her son's most unfortunate end.

Chapter 22: Signs of the Times – in France, 1945

Our mess sergeant makes an announcement: "Men, do not dump your cigarette butts on the left-over food before dropping it in the clean garbage drum." He states that a farmer picks it up for his pigs. I would not be surprised if no pig ever came within smelling range of that can.

A railroad track. Locomotives are still coal fired. A boy walks along the tracks, carrying a sack. He is looking for coal dropped en passant by the driver of the train. Of course, he cannot take a chance on needing coal sooner than the supervisor expects. He is not the only boy (or woman.)

One of my buddies talks to a French girl who is walking with her girlfriend. She invites him and me for a dinner with her family. They served pommes frites, or French Fried Potatoes. Instead of bringing wine or candy, we bring soap. It is winter. The farmhouse has partitions only for the bedrooms. They have goats. I don't believe I have ever been so happy to leave a place; goats inside smell terribly. I almost was gagging the whole time.

Chapter 23: Paris

Paris was still incomparable Paris as we entered. I do not know if there is any truth in the rumor that Hitler expected Paris to be destroyed, and that one of the German Generals just did not do it. We were staying in the Swedish House in University City. The Metro ran only part of the day, and I walked from U. City to the Church of the Madeleine a number of times. (There was no 24 hour electric service.)

My detachments made history in an operational way. We "confiscated" the use of the Eiffel Tower; we had communications equipment up on the top floor. Of course, we returned the tower in good shape. What else could one do with an Eiffel Tower? Naturally, the public could not ascend the tower during that time.

One of the younger officers was quite amused by this transaction, and I was amused because he thought it was so hilarious.

Chapter 24: Loss of a Large British Bomber

While we were stationed in eastern Belgium, a British Lancaster went down in a wooded area. There was no fire or explosion; the aircraft went down in one piece, with all seven crew members dead. We called higher headquarters, and they told us we would have to take the victims to a cemetery. We asked for volunteers, and easily found the eight men we needed, including myself.

I went with the other men to grave registration at the cemetery. It was extremely muddy there, and we had not been issued overshoes. This was noticed by the grave registration people. One of their men asked us, "Do you guys want overshoes?" We said nothing. He then said,

"You might as well take them, these guys don't need them." This is how we received overshoes.

Chapter 25: Hollywood on Temporary Duty in France and Germany

For perhaps a week, Mickey Rooney ate in our mess hall because, he said, he liked the food there. I had a picture somewhere showing him carrying his mess kit. He was performing at a U.S.O. show in the area. We also had Bob Hope and Jack Benny with a show.

Some time later, at the Jewish New Year 1945, we were in Bad Kissingen, Germany, a rather elegant spa. A chaplain (Rabbi) arranged for services in the "Kurhaus," the official venue of the spa. To everyone's surprise, there was Mickey Rooney, sitting next to Bobby Breen (the tenor, and Elizabeth Taylor's second husband) in the congregation.

The rabbi noticed it, too. His comment: "We have a Kiebitzer here."

Fast forward some thirty years: Mickey Rooney is doing a show in the Oriental Theater on Randolph Street in downtown Chicago. I somehow found his picture and managed to see him in his dressing room. There were two more men in the room, and I showed him the print. He resumed talking to the other men in the room, and I overheard him say that he was in need of a Notary Public, wondering where he could find one. I injected myself into the conversation, informing him that I was a N.P., but that I did not have my seal with me. His answer, "When can you get it here?" "In about fifteen minutes," I replied. In Britain some firms carry the designation "Royal Purveyor." Mine is "Notary Public to Mickey Rooney."

There was also a Danny Kay Show at Mac Dill Airbase, Florida. While in New York City, housed near CUNY on Amsterdam Avenue, I attended a one man show with Jack Benny in a small auditorium at St. Patrick's Cathedral. I was sitting in the first row. His opening line: "You know I am from…" to which I yelled, "Waukegan!" He finished the sentence with, "that's right." No doubt, Jack Benny heard my voice.

Chapter 26: A Different Shower

I believe it was in Northern France where I encountered a unique arrangement. There was a small river, flowing slowly, perhaps six to eight feet wide. A tent was erected over the river, with extra space inside on one bank. Inside was a shower stall with a shower head. Outside was a large garbage drum, with a pump and burning head, connected to the fuel source. The system worked very well; I saw this type of shower only once. The shower was used by infantry men who were quite surprised when we showed up with the 9th Air Force insignia on our uniforms.

Chapter 27: Jalhay, Belgium

We were stationed in a small town, not too far from the German border, for most of the third quarter of 1944. It was located not far from Verviers, a city with a population of perhaps 80,000 residents.

We took over a small school house, quite primitive, with a privy outside. We had "captured" an Opel bus which we converted to serve as company orderly room. We had also taken the small restaurant across the street which served as our mess hall. A number of things worth reporting happened while we were there. The Germans started sending rockets from a North Sea port in our direction. Its name was V-1, but we called it the "Buzzbomb." The first time it flew over us it made the building shake, and we could not fathom what it might be. Later on we discovered more of the details about it. It flew over, rather low, with a loud noise, similar to an airplane. At a certain point, when it was past you, the motor stopped, and about ten seconds later it exploded. The danger was – if the rocket's noise cut out before reaching you, you might be in the explosion zone. I do not believe that there were many casualties from it, but it was an effective psychological weapon. It kept everyone somewhat edgy. We suffered through it for a number of months, in many locations in Belgium.

At one time we took over a beautiful mansion, not far from where we housed in Jalhay. The main parlor had plate glass windows; it was gorgeous. One morning we discovered that the place had changed dramatically. A buzzbomb had gone off about a thousand feet from the building. At one time I was out on an errand. When returning I saw that a buzzbomb had hit in the center of the intersection which I had crossed. I had to drive around a huge crater.

Then a most regrettable event happened. Liege, the larger city not far from Verviers, was known as the old city of gunsmiths. As we got closer to Germany, a rumor circulated that when we would enter Germany, we had to be armed, i.e. carrying our carbines. A number of men, including the officers, went into Liege and bought small 9mm pistols; they were rather inexpensive. We were having visitors at that time – the commanding officer of the squadron, a colonel, and the executive officer, a major, who had also bought one of the pistols. It seems the major was not careful. The gut of his pistol had a bullet in it, and when he showed it to the colonel, it went off. Luckily, no vital organs were injured. Our first aid team took over, and the colonel arrived in the hospital not long after the shooting. Of course, this was grist for everyone's mill, while musing how battle scarred GI's might react when they exchanged experiences. As one can imagine, the relationship between the two officers was never quite the same. I would surmise that neither officer ever joined the N.R.A.

The counterweight to the above story is a happy event. There was a marriage between one of the men, about 30 years old, and a young Belgian 18 year old girl who had had a very sheltered upbringing. The wedding took place in a nice restaurant in Verviers, a provincial capital. There was no other such event. As there was some paperwork to do, I was invited. It was a very nice affair. Wild boar was served. I wound up sitting near the Catholic chaplain who was very good company.

It was interesting to see that a near normal life was conducted in Verviers. There was a legitimate theater, and they were performing a musical. It was a nice change from our simpler life in the past months. Some time in December of 1944 we were told in case of any hostile action we should immediately report in person to a certain office, perhaps a half hour's drive from us. We were supposed to dry-run the route, so that in the excitement we would not miss the place. One morning some of our men found green German parachutes nearby. At once I went to the designated place – however, the Army unit there had left. Our unit left within a few hours for the western part of Belgium. This was the beginning of what would later come to be known as the Battle of the Bulge.

Chapter 28: Town of Eu, Belgium

Eu, Belgium was home of the Reverend Georges Pire, the 1958 Nobel Peace Prize Honoree. It was also a much appreciated place for an overnight stay.

One of the important "rituals" in the Army is the payroll. The procedure is as follows: the number two noncom in the orderly room (the unit office) types the payroll, listing all names, grouping them by ranks, and filling in the relevant information. Every man has to place his signature next to his name, assuming he checks and agrees with it. In reality, all he can possibly check is that his name is placed at the proper rank. As a practical matter, if for some reason the person is not available, someone else signs it. It is not possible to hold up the payroll for one man, when 120 men must be paid on time. The payroll then is taken to the nearest official Finance Office, with a Finance Officer who is either a Major or a Captain. Staff makes the proper computation, requests the funds in proper notes and change, and takes it to the respective group's location.

We had two sites, the main one and one forward site, about twenty miles further out. An officer is not permitted to drive cars in the Army except in emergencies. So it happened that on a cold snowy winter day I had to drive the Captain to the forward site, the immediate reason being that about a dozen men needed to sign payroll. By the time I was supposed to return with the Captain, plans had changed. The Captain and the Major went back in a different Jeep with a new driver. I was assigned an old Jeep, with an enclosure (homemade, in bad shape and in need of repair), and also given the Major's heavy and voluminous baggage. I was told to drive by myself. By the time I left, it was almost dark. My route took me west, through Liege, and from there about another forty miles. Of course, there were no headlights on the Jeep – only very dim lights called cat eyes. The first part of the trip came off well; I stayed close to a convoy of medical trucks, and was able to keep on the road. It had started to snow heavily. However, the convoy turned off on a side road. I could hardly see the road, and was narrowly avoiding going into the ditch. However, there was salvation in sight. I entered a small town called Eu, with a well-lit schoolhouse that U.S. soldiers had occupied. Right there and then I said to myself that the war was over for the day.

There was a big job yet to be done. I had to move the Major's baggage into the building lest it be stolen. I also had to remove the rotor from the distributor, because the Jeep had no keys and I planned to stay overnight. My baggage included a folding cot. To my surprise, the schoolroom I entered was occupied by men sleeping on the floor, rather embarrassing for me as I carried my cot through the door. Well, they had seen the cot anyway, so I decided I might as well be comfortable. Duty bound, I called the Captain and explained my delay, to his relief.

Luckily my return trip was uneventful. No doubt the Captain was glad to see me, not just because the Jeep had no fender damage. Thus ended a junior Erlkoenig Winterreise (the sick Jeep instead of the child.)

Chapter 29: A Case of Duress – Nice Try!

I was instructed to take the courier run to Headquarters IX Tactical Air Command. My vehicle was an old Jeep with a wooden homemade top which was loose and made a lot of noise. Besides, the two-lane road was in bad shape, making things worse. About halfway, a number of assorted vehicles rolled towards me, and I noticed that some men were waving their hands. Realizing that they were not just being friendly, I pulled to the side and looked the Jeep over. I had a flat tire, which due to the condition of the Jeep and the road I had not noticed. Somehow I completed my run and the Jeep was taken to the motor pool.

This is what is known in Army circles as GPLD – Government Property Lost or Damaged. When someone breaks a plate in the mess hall, there is most certainly going to be one man who hollers "GPLD!" If the soldier is held responsible, a statement of charges is prepared and the amount is deducted from his pay until paid. Our supply room had two men – the Supply Sergeant and his assistant.

Shortly after the loss of the tire, I noticed that the assistant quite often came to my office, asking me to type up forms for him. After the number of such requests increased dramatically, I realized that I had to put a stop to it. So when he came in again with a few forms I said, "Listen, I have my own work to do. I have no time to do yours, too." His reply: "Then I will make out a statement of charges for the tire." It was time for a haymaker, as I knew he would not fill out the form without me. I replied, "You could not do it without me." End of story – a triumph of virtue.

An interesting angle regarding IX TAC, or Ninth Tactical Air Command: An Army unit captured a German fully automatic telephone system made by Mix & Genest, a German manufacturer. My unit was asked to translate an instruction book. We were fortunate in having a technically capable person who knew German very well. The system was installed, and it is a fair assumption that not many headquarters had such equipment. Incidentally, that buddy of mine, the technician, is alive at 91, living in Staten Island, NY, and I am in touch with him.

Chapter 30: Yes Virginia, There is a Spa in Belgium

The winter of 1944-45 was the most severe winter in many years. When we entered the real Spa, the weather had improved considerably. It boasted quite old fashioned splendor – but still beautiful. And we did take baths there in real old-fashioned bathtubs.

Chapter 31: Death of F.D.R.

F.D.R. died on April 12, 1945. That day found us in Marburg, Germany, a city of about 80,000 with a world-famous university which has bragging rights for Nobel prizes. We were housed in a building which used to be a school for girls with problems. As I got up in the morning, one of the men had received a wire from the Associated Press about the President's death. This was a big surprise, and was posted on the bulletin board.

It was also the place where I ran into a Nazi nurse fully equipped with Nazi insignia. The guard informed me that a woman in a white nurse's uniform wanted to speak to me. I went outside to the gate and saw the woman displaying an official badge with a swastika. I was so upset that I could hardly speak; I told the guard to ask her to remove the badge before I would talk to her. She complied, and upon speaking with her I learned that she had only a minor request.

Chapter 32: A Rebuilt Synagogue and Pope Benedict XVI

At Passover time in 1945 we were stationed in a little town west of Cologne, Germany. The Jewish chaplain contacted me and told me that he was going to conduct Passover morning service at a synagogue in Cologne. That synagogue surely had a checkered past. It was burned down in early November of 1938 by the Nazis, with only the basic walls standing. Then it was hit either by British or American bombs in the war. There were perhaps a dozen Jewish people in the area, having been in hiding during the Nazi era. Matzah, unleavened bread, were procured for distribution. And since the Rabbi's knowledge of German was rather meager, he asked if I would deliver a short sermon, mainly reflecting hope and help for the Jewish families in the area.

In the years following the war, the synagogue had been rebuilt, with the help of many German government agencies. It was by chance that the Pope selected that synagogue to be the first he would visit in his native Germany in the summer of 2007. When the media reported on his travel plans, I wrote to the synagogue telling them of my connection while stationed in the Cologne area, and of my part in the synagogue's history. I asked to be invited, as attendance was by invitation only; they complied. I traveled by myself at the age of 92 to Germany, my native country. Security was very tight. Hours before, there were guards and police on the surrounding streets, and access was limited. There is now a memorial at the point of entry of the Pope. He spoke in

German for a good half hour. It was a powerful message, and he used no euphemisms in describing the events of the twelve years of Nazi rule. After the Pope's address, lunch was served. A great many Cardinals were present, as well as many government officials. The Pope was not present at the lunch, as he had returned to the local Cardinal's residence.

Chapter 33: Visiting My Father's Grave

When my unit was about 150 miles from Nuremberg where my father is buried, I realized it might be my only chance to visit my father's grave. I mentioned this to the commanding officer of the detachment. He authorized a Jeep and a driver, and also an overnight stay in an Army transit place. At the Jewish cemetery in Nuremberg I met a man whom I had known while living in that city. He had become the caretaker of the cemetery. He was married to a Christian woman; this kept him off the deportation schedule, although toward the end of the war with the large number of German casualties he felt that he was at risk.

The City of Nuremberg, together with its twin city, Fuerth, had a population of about half a million. It was heavily damaged, many areas virtually destroyed. There were some which I could not identify. However, almost miraculously, the old city with its many historical sites was not as badly damaged. These sites were either not affected, or damaged in a way that made it possible to restore them. Among large cities, Nuremberg is probably the one with the largest number of such areas. The cemetery was ringed by a freight railroad spur. One corner was bombed by a fighter plane, an event that damaged about twenty graves. My father's grave had a standup marker which had been toppled by vandals. I had a carton of cigarettes, which had cost me 50 cents. Every man was entitled to buy one carton once a month; cigarettes were really our unofficial currency. I used the carton to pay for restoration of my Father's grave marker. This was the first time I visited my father's grave in eight years, and I was quite shaken up, seeing my father's grave vandalized.

My father took sick in May of 1935, and passed away on July 12 of that year. He was never hospitalized. We had a private nurse during his last weeks. Some years after returning home from my Army service, I wanted to know why he was not admitted to a hospital. Were his lack of hospitalization and subsequent death the result of discrimination against Jews? In response to my inquiry to the chairman of the city council, I was informed that while there was no written policy denying Jews admittance to the city's hospital at that time, it was possible that they were just not admitted as a matter of practice. Even without a written policy, it may have been the unofficial policy.

Incidentally, Alfred Dreyfus (whose case rattled Europe in the late 19th Century) died within a day of my father.

On the way back we stopped briefly at a town of 25,000 called Kulmbach, where we had lived before moving to Nuremberg in 1921. Incidentally, Kulmbach has three breweries. The brand of one of them is available in the United States. The purpose of our stopping in Kulmbach was to take a picture of the house where I had lived. I imagine that if we were observed taking a picture of just one house we could have left a lot of worried people in our wake. Not surprisingly, the house did not look quite as impressive as I remembered it.

Chapter 34: Weimar and Buchenwald

Weimar was, and still is, a beautiful city. Before World War I it was the capital of a regional prince with his official residence. For some time it was also the home of Schiller and Goethe. It is perhaps ironic that outside this type of city the concentration camp of Buchenwald was located.

My unit was not part of the Army which liberated the camp. We, most likely, arrived there the day after. The camp itself had not been cleaned up yet; there was a stench and the ground was quite muddy. The prisoners were still in their "beds," many layered wooden shelves. The United Nations Relief Organization (UNRA) was in the process of moving the prisoners to other camp facilities.

What we saw at the concentration camp left us all shaken up.

Chapter 35: It Still Sounded German

Kassel, Gemany.

The war was over when we moved into a permanent headquarters for armored divisions. We found a room suitable for three men. The sign on the door showed three German sounding names. We took the sign off and replaced it with our names: C. Kohlmeyer, W. Leffler, H. Schueftan. Not much of a change! During the war, we had to park trucks parallel to buildings, so that they would be less visible from the air. To my horror, I discovered in the morning that someone had parked a car perpendicular. Then it hit me: "THE WAR IS OVER!' One gets adjusted even to war.

Chapter 36: In Vino Veritas

The war in Europe was over and some of the men were making preparations to go home. There was a man from upstate New York, with about four years service, and about thirty-eight years old. He at times made snide remarks to me, and I had the feeling he did not like me. Of course, that is his right.

A number of men were in a large room inside a building; they were imbibing. The man from upstate New York was thinking out loud: "I have been dreaming about going home for many years, and now when it is about to happen, I don't really know how to feel about it. I have a lot of good friends, and I am used to this kind of life." Then he turned to me: "You, Henry, are one of the good guys in this outfit, and everybody knows it, too." I do not think that I have ever been as surprised as I was that time. It appears one cannot trust one's judgment all the time.

To some extent, I felt the same way he did about going home. I had applied for a rank called 'Warrant Officer," similar to Lieutenant, and passed the written exam with a score of 98.5 and also the interview by a board of officers. But then the Army stopped appointments to W.O. Had I been appointed, I might have stayed in the Army. However, I did not want to stay in as a non-officer.

Chapter 37: A Personal Pilgrimage

It was a Sunday afternoon, after the war in Europe had ended, when I received a number of messages from SHAF, Supreme Headquarter Allied Forces. One message informed us that men having immediate family members in the British mandate Palestine would be able to apply for temporary duty at a leave center there, for ten days plus travel time. I immediately typed up my application, the captain signed, and the currier left for Frankfurt the same day. My application, as well as that of another buddy, were approved. Applications received later were rejected. We took the train to Paris and boarded a flight at Orly Airport. To our surprise, we were bumped off in Rome; we had a very low priority. We were instructed to stay overnight at a U.S. Army Transit Camp, and report to Ciampino Airport every morning, staying until 4 PM. The first morning we settled down for a good cup of coffee in a little snack bar, we had an unpleasant surprise. Our destination had been declared off limits for U.S. Army Personnel. Well, we went into a huddle and decided – as we were already in Rome – to keep going. We could do only limited sightseeing; we saw St. Peter's Cathedral only from the air, coming in very low. On the fourth day we got on a flight of 150 miles, to Naples. There the same process repeated itself. The next flight took us to Athens, Greece, where we changed to a DC-3 bound for Cairo, Egypt. Of course, in Cairo the moment of truth had arrived. We saw an officer at a Middle Eastern Command. He confirmed that the area was off limits, but, he advised us, as we were already there, to return in about a week. There was again a U.S. Transit Camp.

Walking around in downtown Cairo, we noticed a familiar sight which made me feel more at home, a conventional sign at a camera store with the logo "HORNSTEIN." Soon after, our group of two men increased by one, as a U.S. Army lieutenant asked to join. While we were discussing what to do next, a local 15 year old boy started talking to the Lieutenant, and hold him that he was a boy scout. He also offered to help us with the sights, and the officer accepted. Well, my needs of visiting mosques were amply covered, even for a life as long as mine. We probably saw five of six of them. My friend and I kept nagging the officer to find out what the boy would charge. His response, "Don't worry!" After about two hours our guide took us to a bazaar, "To do some shopping," as he said. At that point I whispered to the Lieutenant, "Give him about $5.00," and he agreed. Arriving there the boy talked to one of the vendors, then turned to us and told us that he had to go his way, and that we owed him $20. For 1945, this was an exorbitant amount. For comparison, at the time I think I made about $40.00 a week. A U.S. Senator was paid $10,000 per year. The officer paid silently, not looking happy at all. My buddy and I did not contribute.

I wound up taking the Nile boat ride, and going to the Pyramids. I entered one of the Pyramids; it was quite interesting. Another thing seen from the Nile River: a mill driven by a donkey going around in a circle. Not a new invention. The general area also offered camel rides, and I couldn't resist. My lesson from doing so: my Army Jeep had better springs, and one does not mount a camel from a ladder. The camel seemed to be double-jointed in his forelegs. He kneeled, and when he got up, I suffered a minor earthquake! There is an old German saying, most likely hundreds of years old, "When someone goes traveling, he has things to tell." Still as true as ever.

The following week we were informed that our travel had been approved, at our own risk and expense, by train from Cairo to Jerusalem. That route ran via Ismailia and Gaza. The route has not been running now for many years, and the tracks have since been removed. Arriving at our destination, we found out that the Leave Center no longer existed. It was a joyous reunion; both my sister and brother had gotten married during our time apart, and there were nephews and nieces.

This train again took us to Cairo. As there was damage to the rail line in Palestine, caused by Jewish troops, there was a curfew at 8:00 PM. My train left at 9:00, so my brother could not see me off at the station in Rehovoth. On the way, something unusual happened. There was a station in Gaza which turned out to be a rest stop. There were approximately six wooden huts, restrooms, which were marked by the British with the name of the specific group which could use them, divided up based on gender and skin color.

There was no comparison between going there and returning; I boarded a plane in the morning, stopped for refueling in Rome, and was in Paris at midnight. As fringe benefits go, this certainly was a great one. I had been absent from the detachment for more than five weeks.

Chapter 38: The German Dentist Before Denazification

This happened in 1945 when the war was over. We were stationed in a little town not far from Frankfurt. I had broken off part of a tooth, and I did not want to deal with the Army dentist, because they usually extracted such teeth. It was easy enough to find a dentist, so I made an appointment and told him that I would like him to cap the tooth. There was no problem except for one item – he had no Novocain. "Can you stand a little pain?" he asked. I assured him that I could. Needless to say, it was not a little pain. It was torture, and moreover, the tooth was a live tooth. He stopped every few minutes while his assistant put a cold washrag on my forehead.

I was rather angry later on; had he told me that it was going to be quite painful, I could have gotten the

Novocain quite easily from a medic, for perhaps a five dollar bill. I showed up for the appointment to get the cap installed, but there was another big problem. The curtains were drawn at the office, the dentist did not wear his white coat, and the assistant looked quite unhappy. He had been informed by Military Government to stop practicing until his political past had been investigated. He had informed the Military Government that he had a U.S. Sergeant as a patient, and that he needed to finish the work. He received permission to install the cap on my tooth and completed the job, which, as it turned out, was good for many years. However, this episode had a much deeper meaning for me. Having lived in Germany during the years when Jewish professionals were forbidden to practice, all I could think was that I had lived to see the reverse happening.

Chapter 39: Our Last Stop in Germany

Bad Vilbel, north of Frankfurt, was my last station in Germany. The war was over, we had no mission, and things were a little on the boring side. Frankfurt presented some diversion; a few of us walked about two and a half miles before catching a Frankfurt streetcar which would take us to places within the city. There were reports that one U.S. soldier had been shot walking the same route. From then on we got approval to use a Jeep. I would like to mention also that Frankfurt did not have the damage which I saw in cities like Nuremberg or Kassel.

Chapter 40: Going Home Step #1

When the mass exodus from Europe to the United States began, the Army built a number of camps in the LeHavre, France area. They had the names of popular cigarettes: Camp Phillip Morris, Camp Tareyton, etc. With cigarettes now having lost their good name, it could never happen today.

We left from Frankfurt in an electrified train; it changed to an old coal-driven engine at the French border. It was a cold winter day. The train was comprised of day coaches, and I was in the last coach. We discovered that the last car was an old crew car, and some of my buddies and I took it over. It is a truism in the Army that if someone finds something good, there are always volunteers ready to do the work in the hope that there will also be something in it for them. Along this vein, someone found a stove, there were volunteers, and we were riding in warm comfort. I wound up in Camp Herbeert Tareyton where I ran into an old boyhood friend on his way home; I had tried, without success, to meet him in Germany for about a year. He and I did not return on the same ship. I stayed at Camp Tareyton for about five days.

Chapter 41: SS Frederic - 12,000 Tons

As ships go, this ship was modest, small, and quite subject to the rigors of the wintry North Atlantic. It turned out to be a safe trip, but it was not pleasant. IT was not a good ride, and a great many of the men were seasick. I did not get sick, but I did have what is known as dry heaves a few times. Yet I was still better off than most men; I had hardly boarded the ship when there was an announcement:

"Wanted – Man to play records and to make announcements."

For a man who was limited service at one time, I moved pretty fast to claim that job. Success! There were a number of benefits. I was permitted to sleep on a couch in the Audio Room in the center of the ship, instead of in a hammock in the lowest level of the ship where many men stayed up into the wee hours of the morning gambling and playing cards. I also did not have to stand in the chow line for meals. It was a safe trip home, and I was happy to be going home.

Chapter 42: Your Dog Will Always Know You

When we were in Belgium, the First Sergeant, who had become a very good friend of mine, bought a German Sheppard dog, a female named Totache. The dog had two masters; she minded both her owner and me.

The first Sergeant lived in Cincinnati, Ohio. When I was back home in Chicago, I spent one weekend at his house. He told me that he had somehow managed to take the dog home on the ship. It seems that he was not an effective guardian of a female dog, as some time after getting home, Totache had a litter of two. He kept her son. It is interesting what happened when I saw Totache for the first time. First she made an unfriendly noise, then - like switching gears – she wagged her tail. It was a reunion.

Her son looked like a purebred.

Chapter 43: No 90 Day Wonders There

Newspapers sometimes wrote about people who were promoted, as officers, very quickly. There was a cartoon in a magazine, I remember, showing a doorman in front of a nightclub in a very fancy uniform. A guest entered, saying to him, "I see you are back in uniform, Admiral!"

In contrast, in my Army life, I dealt with a distinguished group of officers. There was A.J. Copp, a pianist and entertainer who worked with Lena Horn. There was H.T. Silverstein, a tenured professor of 18th century English literature at the University of Chicago, and Lauren K. Soth who received the Pulitzer Prize for suggesting (in the early fifties) that Russian farmers come to Iowa to view our farming methods, and who later became editor of the Editorial Page of the Des Moines Register and Tribune.

Epilogue

Looking back at these memories, going back seventy years, it seems as if they contain many varied events, both of a personal and general nature. It can be truly stated that it was not boring. I knew, and also hoped, that my future civilian life would be more sedate – and that is the way it did turn out. I was fortunate, contrary to what the present generation can face, to be employed long-term. Therefore I was truly one of the lucky ones.

I returned to civilian life in Chicago, and worked in accounting. I met my wife at an outing to an Illinois state park. Unfortunately, my wife passed away in 2003, but we were blessed with two children and two grandchildren.

Made in the USA
Lexington, KY
09 October 2016